# WILDLIFE PHOTOGRAPHER

By William David Thomas

**Reading Consultant:** Susan Nations, M.Ed.,
author/literacy coach/consultant in literacy development

**Gareth Stevens**
Publishing

Please visit our web site at **www.garethstevens.com**.
For a free catalog describing Gareth Stevens Publishing's list of high-quality books,
call 1-800-542-2595 (USA) or 1-800-387-3178 (Canada).
Gareth Stevens Publishing's fax: 1-877-542-2596

**Library of Congress Cataloging-in-Publication Data**

Thomas, William David.
  Wildlife photographer / by William David Thomas.
      p. cm.—(Cool careers. Adventure careers)
    Includes bibliographical references and index.
    ISBN-10: 0-8368-8885-5   ISBN-13: 978-0-8368-8885-0 (lib. bdg.)
    ISBN-10: 0-8368-8892-8   ISBN-13: 978-0-8368-8892-8 (softcover)
  1. Wildlife photography—Vocational guidance—Juvenile literature.   2. Wildlife
  photographers—Vocational guidance—Juvenile literature.   I. Title.
  TR729.W54T56   2007
  778.9'32023—dc22                                                  2007027667

This edition first published in 2008 by
**Gareth Stevens Publishing**
A Weekly Reader® Company
1 Reader's Digest Road
Pleasantville, NY 10570-7000 USA

Senior Managing Editor: Lisa M. Guidone
Managing Editor: Valerie J. Weber
Creative Director: Lisa Donovan
Designer: Paula Jo Smith
Cover Photo Researcher: Kimberly Babbitt
Interior Photo Researcher: Susan Anderson

**Picture credits:** Cover, title page © Gavriel Jecan/Corbis; p. 5 © Michael DeYoung/Alaska
Stock; p. 7 © W. Perry/Corbis; p. 8 © Theo Allofs/Corbis; p. 9 © Martin Harvey/Corbis;
p. 11 Daniel J. Cox/Natural Exposures; p. 13 © Oakley Cochran/Alaska Stock; p. 14 Michael
Hortens; p. 15 © Paul Souders/Corbis; p. 17 Michael Fogden/Animals Animals; pp. 19, 20
Daniel J. Cox/Natural Exposures; p. 22 Karel Prinsloo/AP; p. 25 © John Hyde/Alaska Stock;
p. 27 © Denis Scott/Corbis; p. 28 © Stephen Frink/Corbis

Printed in the United States of America

 2 3 4 5 6 7 8 9 10 09

# CONTENTS

Words in the glossary appear in **bold** type the first time they are used in the text.

# CHAPTER 1

# IF YOU CAN FIND IT

*T*ok tok! You are paddling a canoe through a swamp in Arkansas. You feel like a snack bar for mosquitoes. You are looking for an ivory-billed woodpecker. For sixty years, people thought this bird was **extinct.** But in 2004, a man paddling a kayak in this same swamp saw one.

*Tok tok!* Your guide is tapping a stick against the canoe. She is trying to imitate the sound the bird makes when it pecks a tree. You hope the bird will hear it and answer. You slap another mosquito and listen.

*Tok tok!* "Hands inside the boat, quick!" says the guide. You look down. A large water snake is swimming alongside the canoe.

So far, no one has taken a good picture of an ivory-billed woodpecker. A photo would bring you a lot of money. If you can find the bird. If you can get the picture. *Tok tok!*

## Living the Life

You spend two weeks in the swamp. Biting bugs and poisonous snakes surround you. It rains for five days in a row. And you never find that woodpecker. Sometimes, this is the life of a wildlife photographer.

Carefully and quietly, a photographer in Alaska focuses on a brown bear. Getting close to these huge animals is dangerous work.

It's a job that has long hours. It requires great patience. You may spend weeks in deserts, mountains, or jungles. You have to put up with bad weather and rough living conditions. And it can be dangerous. You just can't predict what will happen with wild animals — or in the places where they live.

# Learning the Job

Most wildlife photographers have college degrees. Few actually studied photography, however. Most of them learned by doing it. Many say they learned a lot by studying the work of famous photographers.

Wildlife photographers often start by taking other kinds of pictures. They may photograph baseball games, children, or breakfast cereal. Others begin as a photographer's assistant. They drive the truck to various sites, load the film, clean the cameras, and carry the heavy gear.

This harp seal pup is about two weeks old. Pictures of these animals have helped gain support to protect them.

## The Power of Pictures

Every spring in Canada, harp seals are hunted for their fur. When harp seals are very young, their fur is white. This fur is especially valuable. Hunters don't want to damage the fur, so they don't shoot the baby seals. They beat them to death with clubs. During the 1970s, some photographers took pictures of the hunt. For the first time, people around the world saw what was happening. Because of these wildlife photographs, **protests** began. Animal-rights groups now watch the hunters every year. They try to protect the smallest seals.

Once photographers get a **contract** for a specific job, they begin work. They often do months of research before taking any pictures, however. To photograph an animal, they have to learn about its habits and its home. Being a wildlife photographer is a hard way to earn a living. But most of them love it.

# CHAPTER 2

# IN SAND AND SNOW

S ome deserts are hot and sandy. Some are covered with snow. Interesting animals are found in both — and, of course, so are wildlife photographers.

## Animals Down Under

Australia is often called the Land Down Under. Deserts cover large parts of it. In the daytime, temperatures often reach 115° Fahrenheit (46° Celsius). There is very little water. There are, however, some rare and fascinating animals.

The perentie is the largest of Australia's lizards. These animals eat mice, insects, and even poisonous snakes.

A bilby is one. It looks like a tiny kangaroo with huge ears. Bilbies don't need to drink! They get all the moisture they need from the seeds and insects they eat. During the hot day, bilbies stay underground in deep burrows.

The perentie — also called a goanna — is a big lizard. Some are more than 6 feet (2 meters) long. They stay in underground burrows during the day. Perenties come out at night to hunt.

Photographer David McClenaghan says getting good pictures of an animal requires finding out "what it is, and what are its habits and lifestyle." Getting photos of animals like bilbies and perenties is tricky. One method is to set "light traps" near the burrows. These are lights and cameras connected to wires. When the animals come out at night, they step on the wires. That movement turns on the lights and snaps the picture.

## Desertification

Many of the world's deserts are getting bigger. Scientists call this desertification. It is caused by people and the ways they use the land. The world's population is growing. More and more people are forced to live near deserts. They cut down the few trees there for firewood. Their farm animals eat any plants that grow there. The animals also trample the soil and pack it tight. Together, these things prevent the soil from holding water. Any rain that falls just washes away. The soil dries out and blows away. The land becomes a desert.

Desert photographers must protect their cameras and other gear from sand. The film must be protected, too. Heat can ruin film. And wildlife photographers use a lot of it. A two-week trip may require four to six hundred rolls of film. Desert photography takes preparation, patience, and skill.

## The Snow Leopard

The Himalayan Mountains in Asia are the highest in the world. In the fall of 1973, Peter Matthiessen walked into those mountains looking for a rare animal. Later, he wrote a book called *The Snow Leopard* about his trip.

Almost thirty years later, Ashley Spearing walked into the same snow-covered mountains. She, too, was searching for a snow leopard. But Spearing wasn't a writer. She came to get photographs.

Check out those feet! These young snow leopards have broad paws to walk in snow on the mountains of central Asia.

**Spearing's guides led her to trails** used by the big cats. She set up cameras that detect **infrared beams.** Body heat from animals is given off in the form of infrared beams. Spearing had to think carefully about where to place her three cameras. The same trails were used by wolves, foxes, and sheep. She didn't want pictures of them.

Spearing's careful work paid off. She got more than a dozen photos of four different snow leopards. These pictures will help scientists learn how many snow leopards are left and how they behave.

# CHAPTER 3

# IN FORESTS AND JUNGLES

E arth's forests and jungles are home to thousands of different animals. For much of the year, these places are home to many wildlife photographers, too.

## The Northern Forests

Alaska has whales, bald eagles, wolves, and caribou. But Alaska's most famous animals are its bears. The brown bear is the largest land animal in North America. Some weigh more than 1,700 pounds (770 kilograms). Grizzly bears are almost as big. Both are incredibly strong. Even though they are big, they can move very fast. Photographing them is a dangerous job.

One person who does so is Lisa Anne Selner. She was once a scientist. Then she moved to Alaska and began taking pictures of bears. Now Selner is known as "Grizzly Annie."

Bears have poor eyesight and hearing. But they have a great sense of smell. When Selner is working, she must always know which way the wind is blowing. She must be sure that her scent is blown

A photographer carries two cameras and other gear to capture pictures of a brown bear. Having the right equipment is important when you're out in the wild.

away from the bears, not toward them. If the bears smell her, they may attack.

**A telephoto lens is another must** for photographing bears. These big lenses work like a telescope. Using one, Selner can get a close-up picture of a bear from a safe distance. She also uses some wide-angle lenses. These let her show the bear in its environment. Selner's bear photos often show mountains, rivers, and forests, too.

# How a Camera Works

Light makes a camera work. To get a good picture, just the right amount of light must reach the film. A photographer can control the light in two ways. One is **aperture**. The other is shutter speed.

Aperture is the opening in the camera lens. The opening can be made larger or smaller. Photographers call these openings f-stops.

The **shutter** is a little "door" between the aperture and the film. When it's open, light goes through the lens to the film. Shutter speed is how long that door stays open. A photographer can make the shutter speed faster or slower.

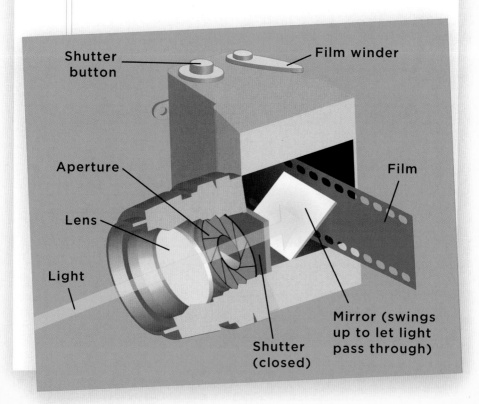

Shutter button

Film winder

Aperture

Film

Lens

Light

Mirror (swings up to let light pass through)

Shutter (closed)

A photographer used a telephoto lens to get this close-up of a mountain gorilla. This **endangered species** lives in the hills of central Africa.

# The Hot, Wet Jungles

Michael Nichols often works for *National Geographic* magazine. He has taken pictures in jungles around the world. Nichols has come face-to-face with gorillas and elephants. He has dodged leopards and poisonous snakes. But sometimes the biggest danger is the jungle itself.

Nichols says, "In the jungle, taking care of myself and my equipment is much of what I do." He carries waterproof boxes. Every night, he packs his cameras, film, and other gear in these boxes. Nichols carries one more important piece of gear. It's a big golf umbrella. "Raincoats and ponchos," he says, "don't keep water off your camera."

# The Rain Forests of Brazil

Wildlife photographers from around the world come to Brazil. This country in South America has the world's largest rain forests. These hot, wet forests are home to one-fifth of all the birds in the world. Thousands of kinds of insects and animals that are found nowhere else in the world live in rain forests. But today, these forests are threatened. Huge areas are being cleared to make room for farms and cattle ranches. Wild creatures of all kinds are dying off because their **habitat** is being destroyed. But the rain forests are important for more than just their wildlife. Rare plants found only in these forests are used to make medicines.

Scientists have called the rain forests "the lungs of the Earth." They give off huge amounts of oxygen. Their trees also absorb pollution from the air. Scientists believe that losing these forests may lead to **global warming** and climate change.

*Hisssss!* This poisonous snake was photographed in the jungles of Malaysia. It is warning the photographer to back off!

Jungles are often dark. Trees and vines grow so thick that you can see only a few yards (meters). Finding animals is hard. Nichols says, "It's mostly going to places the animals go to, and then hiding and waiting." And that's when the bugs get you. Jungles are full of insects that bite. Nichols says, "They bite the most when you're sitting still. If you're in a **hide** trying to do wildlife photography, it's terrible."

# CHAPTER 4

# ON THE PLAINS OF AFRICA

Tsavo is a national park in Kenya, a country in Africa. In Swahili, the local language, *Tsavo* means "place of **slaughter.**" Philip Caputo and Rob Howard went there to get a story. It was about lions — lions that eat people.

## Eyes Like Brass

One day, they drove close to a big male lion. It was resting in the shade of bush. Caputo writes that the lion was "looking at us with eyes that glowed like brass in firelight." Two years before, a lion killed and ate a man near this spot. Was this the same lion?

Howard was lying on the roof of their car, aiming his camera. He stood up to get a better picture. Immediately, the lion focused on Howard. It rose and got ready to charge. Quietly, their guide said, "Say, Rob, might be a good idea to sit down again. Move slowly, though." As soon as he said it, the lion leaped.

Photographers work from the safety of a safari vehicle. Even so, they won't get too close to this rhino.

## Telling a Story

Howard escaped unharmed. But the story says a lot about the work of wildlife photographers in Africa. First, you need a guide. You need someone who knows the land, the animals, and the people. Second, wild animals are always dangerous. Third, you must have a story to tell.

Is this lion just curious, or is it getting ready to attack? Knowing how animals behave helps photographers get better pictures — and keeps them safe.

## Killer Lions

In 1898, the British were building a railroad bridge in Kenya. It would cross the Tsavo River. But over a period of nine months, two lions killed and ate nearly 140 railroad workers. No one would work on the bridge for fear of these lions. The chief engineer, John Patterson, finally shot both of them. The lions were stuffed. They are now in a museum in Chicago. The 1996 movie *The Ghost and the Darkness* tells the story of the lions and the bridge.

## No Snow on Kilimanjaro

Ernest Hemingway was a famous author. One of his stories is called *The Snows of Kilimanjaro*. "Kili," as it is known, is the tallest mountain in Africa. Hemingway wrote that the mountain was "great, high, and unbelievably white against the sun." The white was the snow and **glaciers** at Kilimanjaro's peak. Thirty years ago, snow and ice covered the whole top of the mountain. But today much of the "white" is gone. Global warming is melting the mountain's glaciers. Some scientists think that in just fifteen years, all of Kili's glaciers will be gone.

Wildlife photographers need more than just good photos. They need a good story. The story gives a magazine a reason to buy and use the pictures. Caputo and Howard were taking pictures of lions. But the story they were telling was about people who live near man-eaters.

## Something Different

Every year, thousands of pictures are taken of animals on Africa's plains. Many of them are very good. But to sell, pictures must show an animal in a new or an unusual way.

*Slurrrrp!* These elephants get a cool drink from a water hole. They were photographed in Tsavo East National Park, in Kenya.

Anup Shah found that kind of picture. He and his brother were following herds of zebras in Kenya. Shah writes that one day, the herd passed a giraffe and her calf. The calf was drinking milk from its mother. He says, "A curious zebra came right over to watch. It turned its head with a **quizzical** look to watch the scene. I still remember the amazement on its face while watching the calf."

Photos of zebras are common. So are pictures of a mother and a baby giraffe. But a curious zebra watching a giraffe like a tourist? That is an unusual photo. That's a photo that sells.

## Saving the Elephants

In 1979, there were 1.3 million elephants in Africa. Today, fewer than half of them are left. Some died because farms and towns took over the land where they lived. But most of the elephants were killed for their ivory **tusks.** Ivory can be cut and polished to make piano keys, jewelry, and chess sets. During the 1980s, the tusks from just one elephant were worth as much as $5,000. People killed elephants by the thousands. In 1989, most of the countries in the world signed an agreement. None of them would buy or sell ivory. Far fewer elephants are killed now. Scientists hope their numbers will soon increase.

# CHAPTER 5

# UNDER THE SEA

**P**hotographer Phillip Greenspun said that taking photos underwater has two challenges. First is taking a picture that hasn't been taken by lots of other people. Second is staying alive while doing it.

## Tanks, Cases, and Lenses

Underwater photographers must be experts with **scuba** gear. Their lives depend on it. For cameras, most use the same ones they use on land. They put them inside cases made of special glass or plastic. Buttons and knobs let the photographer control the camera from outside the case. Waterproof cords connect to lights outside the case.

## Water, Color, and Light

Light changes beneath the sea. Water filters out color. The deeper you go, the more colors you lose. In clear water, red is filtered out at 15 feet (4.5 m). Orange goes away at 18 feet (5.4 m). Yellow is gone at 45 feet (13.5 m). Finally, everything looks blue or blue-green. Underwater photographers must be very close to their subjects or use lights to make colors visible.

A killer whale, or orca, can grow up to 30 feet (9.5 m) long. A photographer swam with this whale beneath the cold waters of Alaska.

Nearly all photography under the sea is done with wide-angle or close-up lenses. Most of the time, the camera is no more than 3 feet (1 m) away from the subject. There are two reasons for this. One is that water makes things look closer than they really are. The second reason is color and light. From a distance, everything underwater looks blue and dark.

# Colorful Coral Reefs

Some of the most colorful sea animals live near **coral reefs.** These reefs are found only in warm waters like the Caribbean Sea and Pacific Ocean. Different animals appear on the reefs at different times of the day. Bright orange clownfish — think of Nemo from the movie *Finding Nemo* — are easiest to find in the morning. Moray eels may come out at midday. At night, lobsters leave their holes and walk the seafloor.

There are dangers, of course. Divers must keep checking their air supply. Some kinds of stingrays and sea snakes are poisonous. And naturally, everyone watches for sharks.

## Reef Grief

A coral reef looks like stone. But corals are really tiny living animals. The hard, stony part is their skeleton. When the animal dies, the skeleton remains. Coral reefs create homes for millions of sea creatures.

Today, corals are being destroyed. In some places, a spiny starfish called the crown of thorns is eating corals. But the greatest danger to coral reefs is global warming. When the water is too warm, corals turn white. This process is called bleaching, and it kills or damages corals. Some reefs near Florida are turning white. So are parts of the Great Barrier Reef near Australia. If the coral reefs die, the animals that live there will die, too.

Give me a big smile!  This picture of a great white shark was taken through the bars of an underwater cage.

# Under the Ice

Photographer Nathan Wu wanted something other than warm coral reefs for his underwater photography.  And he got it.  Wu went to McMurdo Station, a U.S. base in Antarctica.  Air temperatures there are often -40° F (-40° C) or colder.

The water beneath the ice is much warmer than the air.  Even so, the water is cold enough to kill an unprotected person in minutes.  Divers must wear heavy underwear, a **dry suit** of thick rubber, and bulky gloves.

Special lights, cables, and controls help this photographer get "up close and personal" pictures of a big grouper in the waters off Florida.

Before Wu could dive, a bulldozer pushed a heated hut onto the ice. A big drill made a hole in the ice about 4 feet (1.3 m) wide. The heat in the hut kept the hole open. If it froze over, the divers would be trapped below the ice.

Wu found that the water was clear and full of wildlife. He photographed sponges, starfish, and octopuses. He took pictures of whales, seals, and penguins, too. He said, "In some places the seafloor is covered . . . with animals."

# Never the Same

Wildlife photography takes you away from home for months. You may have to live in a desert or a wet jungle. You have to face dangerous animals. You may drown or catch a dangerous disease. Why do it?

Annie Griffiths Belt has an answer. She has worked for *National Geographic* for more than twenty-five years. She says it is "knowing that your work has shown someone something and that [he or she] learned something from it." She also says, "The job is never the same, day to day, and it gets you out into the world. It's the most exciting career I could ever imagine."

## Computer Controversy

Computer programs have caused a **controversy** in wildlife photography. Some photographers are using computers to change their pictures. They may place many animals in a picture when the original scene had only a few. They may photograph a bird in a zoo, then put it in a picture of a forest. The pictures are very good, but they are not true to life. Some magazine and book publishers now ask photographers to sign a statement. They must promise their pictures have not been changed on a computer.

# GLOSSARY

**aperture** — a hole behind a camera lens that controls the amount of light that shines onto the film

**contract** — a written and signed agreement to do something

**controversy** — an argument or dispute

**coral reefs** — substances made of coral that have hardened into rock

**dry suit** — a waterproof outfit that traps a layer of air around a diver

**endangered species** — an animal at risk of disappearing forever

**extinct** — no longer living or existing

**glaciers** — huge masses of ice that move very slowly

**global warming** — a scientific theory that Earth's air, land, and water are getting warmer each year

**habitat** — the place where an animal or plant lives in nature

**hide** — a place where someone is hidden from animals

**infrared beams** — heat waves that are given off by people, animals, and other warm things

**protests** — gatherings of people who are objecting to an event, policy, or person

**quizzical** — curious or confused

**scuba** — air tanks and other gear used to breath while under water; the name comes from self-contained underwater breathing apparatus

**shutter** — the part of the camera that opens to expose film to light when a photo is taken

**slaughter** — the killing of large numbers of animals or people

**tusks** — the ivory teeth of elephants, walruses, and other animals

# TO FIND OUT MORE

## Books

*Ansel Adams: America's Photographer.* Beverly Graham (Little, Brown Books for Young Readers)

*Camera.* Great Inventions (series). Larry Hills (Capstone Press)

*George Eastman and the Kodak Camera.* Jennifer Fandel (Coughlan Publishing)

*The Kids' Guide to Digital Photography: How to Shoot, Save, Play With & Print Your Digital Photos.* Jenni Binder (Sterling Publishing Company, Inc.)

*Photography Guide for Kids.* Neil L. Johnson (National Geographic Children's Books)

## Web Sites

**National Geographic Kids**

*kids.nationalgeographic.com/Animals*

Find photos, facts, and videos about various animals on this web site.

**One World Journeys**

*www.oneworldjourneys.com*

Click on "Picturing Our World" or other links to see wildlife photography from around the world.

**Photonhead**

*www.photonhead.com/beginners*

Check out this web site to learn the basics of photography.

# INDEX

# About the Author

William David Thomas lives in Rochester, New York, where he works with students who have special needs. Bill claims he was once King of Fiji but gave up the throne to pursue a career as a relief pitcher. It's not true. Bill dedicates this book, with fondness and gratitude, to the good people at Gareth Stevens in Milwaukee. *Vinaka vaka levu. Moce mada, i tau.*